Our
Christ-Centered
Faith

A Brief Summary of
New Testament Teaching

By
J. C. Wenger

HERALD PRESS
Scottdale, Pennsylvania
1973

OUR CHRIST-CENTERED FAITH

To Ruth

Foreword

In this booklet I have attempted to set forth clearly and succinctly some of the major doctrinal emphases of the New Testament as understood in the Free Church tradition — commonly called the Anabaptist-Mennonite tradition. I have relied on such major interpreters of the sixteenth century as Conrad Grebel of Switzerland, Michael Sattler of South Germany, Pilgram Marpeck of the Tirol, Obbe and Dirck Philips of Friesland, and the Frisian Menno Simons who served largely in what is now North Germany.

One cannot understand the Anabaptists unless he realizes that they sought only to direct all men not to their own ideas and concepts, but to Christ and His Spirit-led apostles — that is, to the writings of the New Testament. The Free Churchmen made wide use of the Old Testament, to be sure, but they interpreted even Moses and the prophets christologically. They would have endorsed Augustine's aphorism: "The New is in the Old contained; the Old is by the New explained."

Those who wish to read further are directed to the four-volume work, *The Mennonite Encyclopedia,* and the literature cited at the close of each article. Here one may read on any doctrine or leader, on any major city, province, or land related to the Free Church tradition.

In the spirit of the sixteenth-century Anabaptists I sincerely appeal to the reader to test what I have written for its faithfulness to the teaching of the New Testament, and to accept only that which rings true to Christ and His Word.

J. C. WENGER

Eastern Mennonite Seminary
Harrisonburg, Virginia 22801
April 3, 1972

Contents

Introductory

Apostolic Christianity

First-century Christians were a happy people. They believed that the Son of God, His "Word," had become incarnate in the person of Jesus of Nazareth, and that this divine Person, the God-Man, had died for their sins, had arisen from the dead, had ascended to the Father, had baptized them with the Holy Spirit on the day of Pentecost, and that He would come again for them on the Last Day. These believers went everywhere, telling people of Christ the Savior, and those who were willing to turn from sin and put their trust in Christ, they baptized with water, thereby inducting them into God's covenant people, the Christian church. They taught a simple plan of salvation: that whoever calls on the name of the Lord Jesus will be saved. Salvation is by grace through faith.

The church was a brotherhood of those who by personal conversion were loyal disciples of Christ. These disciples had been "born again" by the Word and the Spirit of God. The church was characterized by simplicity of organization — being led by men called overseers or elders, and assisted by dedicated servants called deacons. Each local assembly of the believers met together frequently to "remember the Lord" in the holy and joyful service of the bread and the cup. In the course of time this holy celebration came to be called the "Eucharist," a Greek word meaning thanksgiving — for the Christians were deeply grateful to God for providing salvation through Christ. Spiritual guidance was given to each assembly by the Holy Spirit as He illuminated the hearts of the believers, and as He spoke through human spokesmen called prophets. Christ's twelve apostles, soon augmented by a most effective leader, Paul, also gave valuable leadership to the church.

Catholicism Emerges

Little by little a hierarchy developed, and the brotherhood character of the Christian church was gradually lost. Ordained men came to be thought of as "priests," men with divine powers not possessed by the "laity." And the church itself became a worldly organization, no longer being a happy brotherhood of earnest disciples of the Lord Jesus. Eventually both individual men and women withdrew into the desert to live a life of holy contemplation and prayer. The monks began to live communally in what were called monasteries, and the nuns in cloisters.

The last major persecution of the Christians ended in 313, and in 380 Christianity became the official and required religion of both the Eastern and Western empires. By 600 the papacy had evolved. Eventually the number of sacraments was established as seven. The twin doctrines of purgatory and of indulgences were developed. Unbaptized babies were assigned to the "limbo" of the infants, and forever denied the sight of the face of God.

All sorts of ceremonies were developed, such as making the sign of the cross, the use of holy water, holy ashes, holy oil, holy salt, and so on. Prayer was offered to angels, to various departed "saints," and especially to Mary, who was honored with the title "Mother of God." The doctrine of the baptismal regeneration of infants was simply assumed. Eventually the cup was withheld from the laity, and the congregation received communion in "one kind" — only the consecrated wafer, which was regarded as Christ Himself. Priests and bishops were required to remain unmarried. And worst of all, all this unbiblical development was declared to rest upon the "tradition" of the church — which was regarded as of equal authority with Holy Scripture, and was held to have been entrusted by Christ to His apostles, especially to Peter and those who since that time sat in his chair at Rome. The popes not only waged war on various occasions, just as other worldly rulers; they even promoted holy "crusades" to seize possession of the Holy Land from the Turks, encouraging armies to slay the "unbelievers" (Muslim monotheists). Many Jews (also monotheists) were also slain.

Sixteenth-Century Protestantism

Martin Luther and the other sixteenth-century Reformers made a desperate attempt once more to bring the church back to the apostolic doctrine. Luther taught only two sacraments, baptism and communion. He believed the central doctrine of the gospel to be righteousness by faith — he liked the phrase, justification by faith. He vigorously repudiated the papacy. He encouraged monks and nuns to marry and to return to a normal life in society. He taught the priesthood of all believers. He rejected tradition as a coauthority with Holy Scripture; his slogan was, "The Bible only." The debt of all Protestants to Luther is great. Zwingli taught similar doctrines in Switzerland, Calvin's Reformed theology was influential in France and the Netherlands, John Knox was the father of Scotch Presbyterianism, and Thomas Cranmer brought the Protestant Reformation to England.

The Free Church

In addition to Roman Catholicism and Protestantism there was in the sixteenth and subsequent centuries a third type of Christianity known as the Free Church. Among its leaders were Conrad Grebel and Felix Mantz of Switzerland, Pilgram Marpeck of the Tirol, Michael Sattler of Germany, and Obbe Philips, Dirck Philips, and Menno Simons of Friesland — as well as the Hutterite Reformers, Peter Walpot of the Tirol and Peter Riedemann of Silesia. All of these Free Churchmen (who objected to the state church — the territorial church system), and various other free-lance Reformers, were lumped together under the scornful and condemnatory term, "Anabaptists" ("Rebaptizers").

The Free Churchmen insisted on separation of church and state, on freedom of conscience and religious toleration, on the saved status of infants and children without any ceremony. They insisted on believer's baptism, on a brotherhood-type church, on a program of setting up disciplined congregations of earnest disciples of Christ, on rejecting the whole corpus of medieval church tradition, and on following carefully the doctrine and way of life taught in the New Testament. They had a Christ-centered Bible. They insisted that the Great Commission of Matthew 28 (calling for missions and evangelism) was binding upon the church of all ages. Their most radical emphasis was on the absolute renunciation of force and violence in human relations; they believed that as disciples of the Prince of Peace they were obligated to follow the way of peace, and even to accept unjust suffering in forgiveness and meekness. They, like the early Christians, rejected military service.

It is with these Free Churches that this book deals.

Those interested in the literature on the Free Church of the sixteenth century should consult the *Bibliography of Anabaptism, 1520-1630,* by Hans Joachim Hillerbrand (Elkhart, Indiana: Institute of Mennonite Studies, 1962), as well as the four-volume *Mennonite Encyclopedia* (Scottdale, Pennsylvania: Mennonite Publishing House, 1955-59). Particular attention is called to "Writings by Anabaptists," the 796 books and booklets listed on pages 121 to 169 of the Hillerbrand bibliography. Representative sources in English include the following:

Conrad Grebel's Programmatic Letters of 1524, Herald Press, 1970

The Complete Writings of Menno Simons, Herald Press, 1966

Enchiridion . . . D. Philip[s], Pathway Publishers, 1966

The Legacy of Michael Sattler, John H. Yoder, Herald Press, 1972

Baptist Confessions of Faith, William L. Lumpkin, Judson Press, 1959

Bloody Theatre or Martyrs Mirror, T. J. van Braght, Herald Press, 1951

Account of Our [Hutterite] Religion . . . Peter Rideman, Plough Publishing House, 1970

The best general history of the Anabaptist-Mennonite churches is *An Introduction to Mennonite History*, edited by Cornelius J. Dyck,

Herald Press, 1968. The finest summary state-
ment of the essence of Anabaptism is Harold S.
Bender's *The Anabaptist Vision*, Herald Press,
1944.

A New Testament Faith

The Anabaptists, as the first Mennonites
were called in ridicule, did not want to be any
sort of a sect. They desired only to be faithful
New Testament Christians. They wanted to be
regenerated and faithful disciples of the Lord
Jesus Christ, daily bearers of their individual
crosses of discipleship, meek and patient in
tribulation or persecution, winsome witnesses
of the Lord Jesus and His gospel. They wrote
many confessions of faith for the clarification of
their faith before the public and for the edi-
fication of their own members, but they made
little use of any human formulations of doctrine,
ancient or contemporary. Their goal was to be
biblical Christians, in their weakness so filled
with the Holy Spirit that they could manifest
the love of God in all human relations. They
accepted with all their hearts the doctrine of
salvation by grace through faith, but they also
insisted that the Holy Spirit could take weak
sons and daughters of Adam and make them
genuinely Christlike. And for taking the New
Testament so seriously they were written off as
fanatics and hypocrites, and five thousand of
them were destroyed by water, fire, and sword.

1

Christ's Word

Plenary Authority

The entire Protestant Reformation rested on the doctrine of the full inspiration and authority of the Holy Scriptures. And yet in actual practice, tradition was sometimes allowed to stand in the way of a full obedience to the Word of God. The Anabaptists felt that Luther had no right to speak disparagingly of the Epistle of James — Luther did so because James condemned any professed "faith" which did not issue in a life of obedience and good works. Menno called Luther's remarks "bold folly."

Apart from a few liberal Dutch Mennonite theologians after 1860, when the Amsterdam seminary ceased to be fully sound, all theological writers in the Anabaptist-Mennonite tradition from Conrad Grebel (d. 1526) to Harold S. Bender (d. 1962) held to a high view of the Scriptures. The theologians of other traditions were either puzzled or annoyed at the utter simplicity which dared to take in simple faith such "hard sayings" of Christ and His apostles as not to lay up treasures on earth, not to resist an evil man, not to go to law to achieve one's rights, not to swear an oath, and not to use such titles of religious honor as "Father."

Conrad Grebel, the founder of Swiss Anabaptism, declared that he believed the Word "simply out of grace and not from learning." In a letter of 1524 he set the tone for his future church program: he exhorted Muentzer "to seek earnestly to preach only the divine Word and unafraid, to set up and defend only divine rites, to esteem as right and good only what is found in crystal-clear Scripture, to reject, hate, and curse all proposals, words, rites, and opinions of all men, even your own." Again, "Operate only according to the Word, and draw and establish from the Word the rites of the apostles." It was Grebel's conviction that "it is far preferable that a few be rightly instructed in the Word of God . . . than that many through adulterated doctrine falsely and deceitfully 'believe.' " "Press forward with the Word and create a Christian church with the help of Christ and His rule as we find it instituted in Matthew 18 and practiced in the epistles." In brief, "Hold to the Word alone. . . ." "Set up and teach only the clear Word and rites of God, together with the rule of Christ [Matthew 18]."

Similar statements are found in the writings and testimonies of all the major Anabaptist figures: Michael Sattler, Leopold Scharnschlager, Pilgram Marpeck, Dirck Philips, Thomas van Imbroich, and Menno Simons. In defending

17

his Trinitarian faith Menno declared: "I would rather die than to believe and teach to my brethren a single word concerning the Father, the Son, and the Holy Ghost, at variance with the express testimony of God's Word, as it is so clearly given through the mouth of the prophets, evangelists [Gospel writers], and apostles." (See also "Bible" in the *Mennonite Encyclopedia*.)

Holy Spirit Witness

The Free Churchmen took seriously the teaching of the New Testament on the depravity of human nature. They believed that until the Holy Spirit brought conviction for sin to the heart of a person, there was no hope of his becoming a Christian believer. Only the Holy Spirit can bring the individual to repentance and faith. The conversion of everyone coming into the church is a testimony to the effective work of the Holy Spirit in witnessing to the truth of the gospel and the saviorhood of Jesus Christ.

In a similar way, the Holy Scriptures in themselves are unable to bring the sinner to penitence and faith. The entire Bible is, to be sure, the inspired Word of God. But the Holy Spirit needs to operate in the heart and mind of the non-Christian as he encounters the Word — either in its preached or written form — so that it "comes alive" as the living and powerful

Word of God, convicting of sin and pointing to the Savior of the world. In no sense is this a depreciation of the written Scriptures; the lack is not in the Bible. The block is in the cold heart of the unregenerated person reading or hearing the Word. It is the Holy Spirit who gives the "ring of truth" to the Scriptures. This position is set forth in passages such as 1 Corinthians 2 and 2 Corinthians 3. In 2 Corinthians 3:18 we read that we all, as persons having spiritual sight because of the blessed work of the Spirit of God in opening our eyes, beholding the glory of the Lord Jesus on the pages of Holy Writ, are being changed into His spiritual image by the glorious Lord who is [no longer "flesh" but] Spirit. (Compare various versions of the passage.)

Finality of the New Testament

Everybody knows that the Bible has two major parts, the Old Testament which was written prior to the time of our Lord Jesus on earth, and the New Testament which was written after His atoning death and victorious resurrection, and after the ascended Lord had "baptized" His waiting disciples with the fullness of Holy Spirit blessings, beginning at Pentecost. Christians believe that the Old Covenant, made through the instrumentality of Moses, involved holy days, ceremonially clean and unclean foods, animal sacrifices for sin, a priesthood, the rite of circumcision for the covenant people, and the like. The New Covenant dropped the Jewish ritualistic regulations on food, clothing, and holy days; abolished circumcision as a required rite, did away with animal sacrifices and a special priesthood for God's people, instituted water baptism for Christian converts, and set up the Lord's Supper to commemorate the atoning death of the Savior. But the Free Churchmen — in contrast with the state church reformers, Anglican, Lutheran, and Reformed — also understood the New Testament to abolish the swearing of oaths, to call for the nonuse of civil courts to achieve one's rights, and even called for meekness in unjust suffering, including the rejection of force and violence in human relations. In common with the Christians of the first centuries, they refused to serve in the military. (See C. J. Cadoux, *The Early Church and the World,* Scribners, 1925.) These attitudes were commonly regarded in the sixteenth century as pure fanaticism, even a dangerous heresy, for if enough people followed such an ethic, what would happen to organized society? The fact that some of the Anabaptists condemned capital punishment made them still more odious.

The state churchmen stoutly defended the ethical acceptability of the civil oath, the legitimacy of the so-called "just war," and even insisted on the right of the state to crush such heretics as the Free Churchmen on the basis of

Deuteronomy 13, which called for the extirpation of heresy by stoning the offenders. They also rejoiced when the Protestant princes of Germany set up territorial churches — a system in which the state recognized one particular faith as "official," and persecuted dissenters. The Free Churchmen were much displeased with this system, a plan later summarized in Latin as *Cujus regio, ejus religio* (Whose the region, his the religion). The Free Churchmen insisted that in the Apostolic Church era, faith was an individual matter. The state ought not decide for or against any faith. There should simply be religious freedom and toleration. When the Word is proclaimed, some will respond. Those who are born again, "inwardly baptized" with the Holy Spirit, should then be baptized with water and received into the church. The state should neither encourage nor prevent this, but should mind its proper business of maintaining law and order (Romans 13).

The state churchmen recoiled in horror at such concepts and declared that since circumcision was performed on Israel's male infants and since "households" were baptized in the Apostolic Church, infant baptism was proper and right. They accused the Free Churchmen of damning the infants by refusing them water baptism — a charge totally rejected by the so-called Anabaptists. They held, on the basis of Christ's Word, that infants were in the kingdom, indeed the greatest in the kingdom, apart from any ceremony (Matthew 18 and Luke 18). The state churchmen also "exorcised" infants — that is, they had a ceremony to drive demons out of them: a totally superfluous rite, said the Anabaptists. Indeed, the Free Churchmen held that whatever the state churchmen could not prove from the New Testament, they fell back to the Old Testament for, in farfetched analogies or unjustified conclusions — such as the justification of the oath, of infant baptism, of warfare, and of the persecution of religious dissenters. The state churchmen, however, cried, "They are heretics! They reject the Old Testament."

When not in controversy, however, the leading clergymen of the state churches sometimes admitted that their chief differences with the Anabaptists involved such matters as to whether or not infants should be baptized and whether a Christian ought to serve as a magistrate (Zwingli). In 1615 J. J. Breitinger, then head of the Zurich state church, remarked that the Anabaptists "teach faith in God, Father, Son, and Holy Spirit. They do not hold errors which would cause a man to be lost, but such as have been taught by some of the old church fathers."

Christ the Key in Interpretation

The Swiss Brethren, the Austrian Hutterites, and the Dutch Mennonites had a Christ-centered Bible. The Lord Jesus was for them the most important theme of the Old Testament prophetic Scriptures — the Savior or "Messiah" which was to come — and was even more obviously the center of the New Testament Scriptures. On the Emmaus road the Lord Jesus began with Division I of the Old Testament, the writings of Moses; continued with Division II of the Jewish canon (Former Prophets — Joshua, Judges, Samuel, and Kings; and Latter Prophets — Isaiah, Jeremiah, Ezekiel, and the Twelve); and finally went into Division III, which began with its largest book, the Psalms. In all these Scriptures He interpreted to them the things concerning Himself (Luke 24). Seeing Christ as the center of the entire Bible, and making Him the key to its proper interpretation, supported, the Free Churchmen believed, their basic theological and ethical convictions: the saved status of children; baptism as one's sign of commitment to Christian discipleship — indeed, a sort of ordination to serve as His witnesses; the ethic of peace, love, and nonresistance; the nonswearing of oaths; and the like. After sharply reminding one of his theological opponents how he teaches people to fight and retaliate, to imprison and destroy their enemies, "to sentence criminals regardless of whether they repent or not," and to swear according to the law of Moses, Menno asserted forcefully that he himself would teach people (Christians) to use no other sword than that of Christ and His apostles, i.e., the Word of God, to be merciful to penitent sinners, and "scrupulously to stand by their yea and nay," as Christ taught.

Such "christological" interpretation meant seeing the Lord Jesus as both key to, and "Lord" of, the canonical Scriptures. They all witness to Him, and if we are to be faithful we must teach from the entire Bible precisely what He taught. We must understand God's law as He understood it. We must be Christlike, in the power of His Spirit. We must stress what He stressed in theology and ethics. We must treat all people as persons who are precious to God. We must always relate to people, even wrong-doers, as He did: "Father, forgive them, for they know not what they do." Christ Himself left no writings, but He walked with and taught His chosen apostles for several years, baptized them with the Holy Spirit, and promised that He would endow them with "total recall" — so that they might rightly in the Spirit set forth and interpret His teaching, and His life, death, resurrection. Whatever from the Old Testament agreed with and supported the New, was regarded as normative and relevant by the Anabaptists. But whatever fell below the standard of Christ was regarded as pre-Christian, and not God's full and final revelation — such as warfare, divorce and remarriage, polygamy, the oath, deception, and lower status of women, and administration of civil justice by God's children.

2

Christ's Church

Luther's Pioneer Work

To Martin Luther, the lionhearted reformer
of Saxony, goes the honor of discovering afresh
the glorious, liberating gospel of grace through
the Lord Jesus Christ. He was the human in-
strument which God used to make the saving
gospel of Christ known all over Europe. Hu-
manly speaking, had there been no Luther there
might have been no Zwingli, no Grebel, no
Cranmer, no Knox, and no Calvin. Luther was
a mighty theologian, a gifted writer and preach-
er, a hymn writer, a tender family man, a powerful organizer, and a formidable champion of
righteousness by faith — *justificatio* as he called
it in Latin. Luther did not, however, establish
Free Churches. He was content to see the territorial princes set up supposedly Evangelical
(Protestant) churches. The former priests needed help, of course, to begin proclaiming the
gospel of Christ in its original New Testament
form. Luther and his colleagues sought to make
such help available to them. This means, of
course, that Luther allowed the "Constantinian"
union of church and state to stand. (It was the

Roman Emperor, Constantine the Great, whose reign extended from 306 to 337, who took the first steps which culminated a generation later in Christianity being made the official religion of both the Eastern and the Western empires.) Ideally, of course, Luther longed to see a chain of congregations across every territory of Germany composed of those who in "dead earnest" were faithful disciples of Christ. But he did not wish to disturb the territorial church system in favor of Free Churches, so he comforted himself with the concept of the "invisible church" — the true Christians are known only to God.

Grebel's Free Church

Luther likely came to his discovery of "righteousness by faith" about the year 1514 — there is no way to pinpoint the date of his famous Tower Experience. God's Spirit was also at work in northern Switzerland, and by about 1516 Zwingli too was rejoicing in the gospel of God's grace in Christ. Zwingli began his amazing ministry of the Word in Zurich in 1519 and by Passion Week, 1525, was able to inaugurate an Evangelical Lord's Supper in place of the Catholic Mass — the climax of his reform program. In the year 1522 a young married man, an intellectual with six years of university work already completed, Conrad Grebel the patrician, came into the Evangelical circle of Zwingli. Grebel was brightly converted, and

26

really turned from sin to Christ and to earnest discipleship.

By the fall of 1523 he was, however, becoming uneasy about the way Zwingli always seemed to defer to the "Great Council" of the 200 senators who governed Zurich. Zwingli seemed to trust their judgment on determining the tempo of the Reformation. Grebel felt that where the Word of God was clear, we ought to follow it fully, allowing results to God. By the fall of 1524, when Grebel wrote a long letter of 350 lines setting forth his vision of what the Christian church ought to be, he was a convinced Free Churchman. He felt that Christians should be free to share the gospel with those not yet converted. Those receiving the gospel should be free to seal their vows of discipleship by receiving water baptism.

Such converts should organize themselves into fellowships of Christian brothers and sisters — brotherhoods concerned to keep a loving eye on one another and by prayer, counsel, encouragement, and even tears seek to assist one another to be faithful disciples: that is, they must be a disciplined church. The state should grant religious toleration to such Christian churches. Such churches should frequently celebrate their redemption in Christ with holy joy, using the bread and the cup. Simplicity was to be the rule: a simple meetinghouse, a minister dressed simply (no priestly garments), ordinary bread, an ordinary cup, and the only words used in the Lord's Supper should be taken from the New Testament.

Grebel was utterly convinced that the only way to create a faithful New Testament church was to cut loose from the state, and to be once more the kind of church which is described in the New Testament Book of Acts. Zwingli was not minded to turn over the leadership of the Reformation in Switzerland to such young hotheads as Grebel and his colleagues, and saw to it that legal measures were taken against them.

To the credit of both Zwingli and Grebel, however, there was no immediate break. Only after a number of fruitless consultations between Grebel and Zwingli was there a public disputation on January 17, 1525, between the two opponents, each with their loyal supporters, and in the presence of the Council of the 200. The next day the Council ordered all parents to have their babies baptized on pain of exile. But the final straw was on Saturday, January 21, when the Council ordered Grebel and his chief colleague, Felix Mantz, to cease holding Bible study meetings with their followers. The Brethren met to consider the crisis, and felt led of God to organize a Free Church and to inaugurate believer's baptism. They were literally *driven* out of the state church of Zurich. Because all of these folks had been christened as infants, this act of inaugurating believer's baptism was thought of as a rebaptism, and such terms as Anabaptists (in German *Wiedertaeufer* or just *Taeufer*) i.e., "Rebaptizers" were given them as nicknames. In the course of time they were called the "Swiss Brethren" because of the warm spirit of Christian brotherhood in their churches. They themselves avoided the use of all worldly titles, and called one another simply "Brother" and "Sister." Persecution even to death was soon a reality for them. Grebel, however, died of illness the summer of 1526, but Mantz was executed by being drowned in the Limmat River in Zurich the following January.

What Is Christian Baptism?

In the Roman Church water baptism was a sacrament, normally performed by an ordained priest, given to every infant of Christendom to wash away the stain and guilt of Adamic depravity. Indeed, an unbaptized baby was thought to go after death to the "limbo" of such infants for all eternity. The leading Reformers tended in varying degrees to retain something of this theology of infant sin and guilt, and regularly exorcised the demons in such christenings. When Grebel and his Free Church brothers and sisters studied the Gospels and Epistles of the New Testament, they found no justification for infant baptism and for infant exorcism. They found rather that according to the word of Christ

29

Himself, children are without any ceremony already in the divine kingdom. They read in Romans 5 that just as there had been prior to Christ and His redemption a solidarity in human sin, so now in Christ there is a solidarity in redemption. Whatever "guilt" children might have by virtue of being born into the Adamic humanity was by Christ's atonement, they believed, fully removed. Just as the girls of the Mosaic covenant needed no ceremony, and also the boys for the first week, so children now stand in need of no ceremony to insure their salvation.

When boys and girls grow up, however, they do come to the need of a personal commitment to Christ, of conversion from sin to active and conscious discipleship. As they hear the Word of God the Holy Spirit will bring conviction to their hearts. Those who come asking for water baptism, and declaring their faith in Christ the Savior and Redeemer, and their readiness to "walk in the resurrection," are to be joyfully baptized with water, received into the brotherhood, and recognized as commissioned witnesses of Christ and His salvation. The German Bible calls baptism the "Covenant" of a good conscience with God (1 Peter 3:21), and the Free Churchmen thought they could see this theology of baptism all through the New Testament. The water of baptism was, to be sure, not able to save. Only Christ saves. And only those were to be baptized with water who gave evidence of having already been baptized by Christ with the Holy Spirit — they called this "inward baptism." The so-called "sacraments" of the New Testament, such as baptism and Lord's Supper, were not regarded "sacramentally," that is, as being the means of divine grace. It is faith, and faith alone, which lays hold on Christ and His merits. The sacraments were holy celebrations of what we receive from Christ by faith.

"Go Ye Therefore"

The several cantons of Switzerland proved unable to totally suppress the Free Church movement. Fines, imprisonment, and executions were inadequate to crush the hated "Anabaptism." (Oddly enough, their vows of believer's baptism the Free Churchmen had learned from Zwingli, who as late as 1523 was teaching that since infants needed no ceremony to seal salvation to them, it would be a good plan to follow the church of the fourth century, i.e., to institute instruction classes in the Christian faith for "catechumens," and then to baptize them.) Strange as it may seem, the Free Church vision, however, seemed to appeal to many of the Swiss. (Some scholars wonder whether the earlier Waldensian movement in Switzerland might have somehow conditioned the people several generations later to respond to the Free Church missioners.) Dozens of Swiss Brethren congregations sprang up, especially in the cantons of Zurich and Bern. Soon the movement had spread to South Germany and to Austria. In February 1527 an assembly of Swiss Brethren was held in Schleitheim in Northern Switzerland, under the leadership of a gifted minister named Michael Sattler, and the brothers and sisters came to unanimous agreement on a number of major doctrines of the faith. The Schleitheim "Agreement" of Seven Articles had a most wholesome and unifying influence on the brotherhood. It solidified the Brethren on the basic New Testament distinctives for which they stood in a Christendom which had picked up many accretions in the past thousand or more years.

One of the basic New Testament doctrines of the Free Churchmen was personal evangelism. In the New Testament they read of being sent by the Lord Jesus, just as the Father had commissioned Him (John 20:21). And did not the risen Lord commission them to make disciples (Matthew 28:18-20)? It reached the point where it seemed advisable to plan for the evangelization of Europe. Consequently, over sixty representatives of the Brethren from Switzerland, Austria, and South Germany met at Augsburg in Bavaria in August 1527. The Spirit of God led those present to still greater doctrinal unity, and also enhanced their sense of mission in a lukewarm Christendom where vast numbers of people were trusting in sacraments or in a "faith" which did not involve obedient discipleship. It was decided to commission representatives to various parts of Europe: to Basel and Zurich in North Switzerland, to Worms and the Palatinate, to Upper Austria, to Franconia, to Salzburg, to Bavaria. No minutes of the meeting have been preserved. All that we know about it came out in the statements of the participants who were captured during the course of their several missions — men such as Hans Beck, Eucharius Binder, Hans Denk, Leonhard Dorfbrunner, Hans Hut, Joachim Maerz, Gregor Maler, Hans Muttermaier, George Nespitzer, Leonhard Pruckh, Peter Scheppach, Leonhard Spoerle, and Ulrich Trechsel. So many of the missioners were put to death that the meeting had been labeled the "Martyrs Synod." Before the meeting broke up and the several missioners set out to give their witness, a commissioning service was held in the home of Matthias Finder in Augsburg on August 24, 1527.

Oddly enough, the leading Reformers of the sixteenth century saw no place for the Great Commission of Matthew 28. All Europe was already composed of properly christened persons; all that was needed was to bring as many as possible out of the darkness of Romanism into the light of the Evangelical faith. The Anabaptist missioners were thought of as "bootleg" or "hedge" preachers — for they often held their

33

secret and illegal meetings in forests and in caves. And worse yet, they ventured to launch out without proper state authorization as clergymen! The persecution of the Free Churchmen was horribly severe. Many were drowned, more were burned, some were beheaded; and prior to the executions there were often repeated visits to torture chambers. Something of the story of this torture and death is recorded for the Low Countries in the martyrology, the *Bloody Theatre or Martyrs Mirror*, by T. J. van Braght (Dutch, 1660; German, 1748-49; English, 1837). In a general way this persecution was all too successful. For about one generation, the movement grew and thrived. But in a tragic manner, the church gradually weakened under the onslaught, and then ceased to be evangelistic. (This spiritual slumber lasted for centuries, but the Mennonites are once more seeking to recapture the evangelistic enthusiasm of the sixteenth century. Of the 540,000 baptized Mennonites in the world in 1972, about 40 percent are the result of modern mission work in various areas such as Africa, Asia, and Indonesia.)

Menno Simons, a Frisian who united with the Free Churchmen of the Netherlands in 1536, remarked that while the state church clergy rest on easy beds and soft pillows, "we" [Free Churchmen] have to hide in out-of-the-way corners; and while they revel with pipe, trumpet, and lute at weddings and baptismal banquets, "we" have to be on our guard whenever a dog barks for fear an officer has arrived to arrest us.

Faithful Teachers

It might be concluded logically that since all the members of the church were to be faithful witnesses of the gospel of Christ, no clergy were needed at all. But this conclusion did not appeal to the Free Churchmen, for they were trying to set up congregations faithful to the New Testament. And the New Testament does recognize such offices in the church as *overseers* or *elders*, and their helpers, *deacons*. The 1527 Schleitheim *Agreement* speaks of the *Hirt* (shepherd or pastor) who is to function in each congregation, carefully specifying that should he be taken away by persecution, another shall be chosen immediately so that the congregation does not suffer without a pastor. The qualifications given in 1 Timothy 3 for pastors and deacons were to be taken into account in choosing the pastors of each congregation.

It appears that it was not long until a man was first *chosen* for one of these two offices on a probationary basis. If he proved to be faithful and effective he was then *confirmed*. Eventually the confirmed pastors came to be thought of as the ministers with full authority to baptize and give communion, and in some cases were sort of district superintendents: they were called *elders*. Those ministers who assisted them were ministers of the Word or *"teachers"* (i.e., *preachers*). The *deacons* carefully looked after widows, orphans, and the poor, assisted the pastors wherever possible, and often were especially considered the guardians of the peace of the brotherhood; i.e., they sought to effect reconciliation if any tensions developed between members of the congregation. In the Low Countries judicious and spiritual older women were sometimes chosen to render a comparable service among the women of the church; they were called *deaconesses*.

It was considered normal for a minister to continue to earn his own living. He was on the same level as the other members of the church, for it was a brotherhood, not a hierarchy. Yet, since pastors often needed to devote more time than others to the work of the church, as early as 1527 the Swiss Brethren recognized that the church ought to supplement the income of the pastor as needed. Menno was even more emphatic. He urged pastors to rent farms and to milk cows, or to learn a trade. But he also held that insofar as the minister needed help, the brethren would supply it. Menno feared any system that offered a minister exemption from working. He felt that as long as the state churches offer handsome houses and incomes to the clergy, false prophets will appear in droves!

But are the clergy of the Free Churches legitimate pastors, since they lack any sort of state recognition? Yes, declared Menno, their ministry is indeed wholly approved of God. Whenever a man is chosen as pastor by a church with care, and with fasting and prayer, and ordained to the ministry of the Word with the laying-on of hands — following the precedent of the apostolic church — such procedure is scriptural and fully acceptable to the Lord.

A Sharing Community

It will be recalled by those who have read the polemics of the state churchmen against the Anabaptists that said churchmen feared some sort of incipient communism in the Anabaptist camp. (And when the revolutionary Anabaptists did get control of the city of Muenster in Westphalia, and instituted a communism of consumption during the siege of the city by the bishop's army, 1534-35, it seemed to many state churchmen that their suspicions were indeed correct. In all fairness, however, it should be pointed out that a group of peaceful Austrian Anabaptists as early as 1528 adopted a *Christian communal way of life*: initially, to be sure, during the exigencies of a flight during persecution, but permanently as an expression of total sharing and caring in the body of Christ's church. There are still thousands of these devout and peaceful "Hutterites" in North America, living quiet lives of peace and joy in their several colonies — each of which bears the German name, *Bruderhof*.) The Free Churchmen as a whole did not object, however, to the private ownership of property. They farmed or worked at trades to earn a living for their family and to have means to share with those in need. They carried this doctrine of brotherly mutual aid and of Christian helpfulness to the needy so far that many critics misunderstood them as somehow being opposed to the private ownership of property. It must be admitted that the Anabaptists stressed a life of simplicity and frugality to the point that it could actually be acknowledged that they were in very truth opposed to a life of wealth and affluence. The reader must decide whether they were right or wrong in the light of the teaching of Christ and His apostles!

The Anabaptists were critical of the business of being a "middle man" — purchasing products and then selling the products to others. Menno saw in such business grave dangers of dishonesty, of making too much profit. Such merchants are in real danger of being "overcome by avarice" (*Writings*, 369). And every employer must be careful lest he oppress his hired help. He must be careful to give them "decent support." "Do not dock them in their wages," warned Menno. And if an employee has a period of illness, or if he becomes aged and infirm: graciously care for them until their recovery or their death (*Writings*, 365, 366). In other words, what we call capitalism is not in itself evil, but it can easily become an occasion of sin. The Christian disciple needs to master his acquisitive instincts so as to be a good and generous steward. As a Christian disciple he is not even allowed to charge interest when the poor have to borrow. To charge a poor brother interest would be, the Anabaptists insisted, a violation of the "royal law of love."

The Two Kingdoms

The Free Churchmen were pioneers for religious freedom, for the privilege of recognizing Christ and Christ only as the Lord of the conscience. They did not believe in an inclusivist church, with the entire population of an area reckoned as members of the body of Christ because they had been "christened," and holding to a certain faith because the ruler of the area so directed. The whole state church system was an evil of the first order, they insisted. The general population, although obviously not regenerated, considered itself Christian, and resented all evangelism which was directed toward it.

No, cried the Anabaptists, you are not Christ's body! His body is made up of people who have in response to the gracious work of the Holy Spirit turned their backs to sin, voluntarily taken upon themselves the cross of discipleship, decided to pay the cost of being a faithful and obedient follower of the Lord Jesus. The Lord desires, said the Anabaptists, a church "without spot or wrinkle." They knew, of course, that they themselves were accepted by grace, only by grace. But they insisted that only those could be reckoned as members of the church who in their very hearts were eager to know and to do the will of God. Christ does not want, they held, an "invisible church"; He wants men and women, youth and maidens, who in sincerity and truth have given their lives over to Him in love and loyalty. This meant that congregations of disciplined members had to be set up and maintained.

All those who reject the offer of forgiveness and willing discipleship belong to the kingdom of the evil one, or of the "world" — that mass of unregenerated men and women who live in sin and disobedience, who reject the cross of discipleship, who want what a twentieth-century theologian (Bonhoeffer) called "cheap grace" (the blessings of salvation without the cross of discipleship and obedience). When a sinner is converted he is by the Spirit of God transferred out of the kingdom of darkness into the kingdom of God's blessed Son (*cf.* Colossians 1:13).

The state as state is not in the kingdom of Christ. Those are in Christ's church or kingdom who have been born anew by the Word and the Spirit. The church is made up, in other words, of those who have been born again, while the state is composed of all men, both saved and lost. The head of the church is the risen and exalted Christ, while the head of the state is a mere man. The church is controlled by the Word of God, while the state controls men by law. The only sanction of the church is excommunication for continued and unrepentant sin and disobedience, while the state levies fines, uses the threat of force, and imprisons offenders — in some cases even executes them, which Menno thought to be a sin. (If the offender has repented, he is now a brother in the church; if he has not repented, what right does the state have to cut off his opportunity to repent?) The function of the state is to maintain "tranquility and order" (as the German puts it). The state will terminate at the Second Coming of the Lord, while the church will be taken by Christ into heaven for ever and ever. (See the 1527 Schleitheim *Agreement*.)

The Rule of Christ

In Matthew 18:15 the Lord indicated that if a brother sins, one shall go to him alone and seek to bring him back to a penitent and obedient spirit. If not successful, one shall take along one or two others. And if they cannot win the offender, his case shall be turned over to the congregation. And if even the congregation cannot deliver the unrepentant transgressor he must sorrowfully be relieved of his membership in Christ's body or kingdom. This process of seeking to bring each member to full stature in Christ was called *discipline* — the act of helping disciples to be more faithful and obedient to Christ and His Word.

Discipline did not mean making a neo-legalism out of Christianity. On the contrary, Menno stated bluntly that the church does not excommunicate anyone except those who by grievous doctrinal error or by an offensive life morally have already cut themselves off from Christ. One dare not, said Menno, be more lenient or more strict than the Word of God. The brothers and sisters were to make a special effort to cleanse the church of any sin before observing the ordinance of the bread and the cup. This was stated clearly in the Schleitheim *Agreement*, and before observing the Lord's Supper members of the Mennonite Church are still asked: (1) whether they have peace with God, (2) whether they have peace with their fellowmen "as far as in them lieth," (3) whether they have any suggestions for the life and witness of the church, and (4) whether they favor having the communion service as planned.

One finds many references to the "rule of Christ" in early Anabaptism. Conrad Grebel put it this way in 1524: "Press forward with the Word and create a Christian church with the help of Christ and His rule as we find it instituted in Matthew 18 and practiced in the Epistles. Apply it with earnestness and common prayer and fasting, in line with faith and love, and without law and compulsion" *(Programmatic Letters of 1524,* p. 27).

The only point which Grebel stressed even more earnestly than this rule of Christ becomes evident in his vehement denunciation of what he called "false sparing," that is, not teaching people the meaning of costly discipleship, of excusing them from full obedience to all that Christ and His apostles taught, even the so-called "hard sayings" of Christ which demanded turning away from wealth-seeking and from force and violence in human relationships, and which asked Christian disciples to be suffering witnesses for the Lord, even unto death.

Holy and Joyful Celebrations

The Roman Church has long taught that there are seven sacraments: baptism (normally infant christening, involving baptismal regeneration!), confirmation, penance, communion, and the last rites. The two optional sacraments are marriage and holy orders, and one cannot have both. Luther felt that it would be more biblical to speak of two sacraments: baptism and the Lord's Supper, and he insisted also on giving communion in both kinds: the bread and the cup, while Rome had long withheld the cup from the laity — only to once more allow communion in both kinds since Vatican II, 1962-65. The Lutherans, of course, continued to perform marriage ceremonies, to confirm the youth, and to bury the dead with a solemn committal service, but Luther thought it best to reserve the word *sacrament* for the two basic rites which Christ Himself established: baptism and the Lord's Supper. Luther rejected, of course, the doctrine of transubstantiation as taught by Rome, preferring to teach what he called the "Real Presence" of Christ in the communion emblems. Zwingli adopted the memorial view of the Lord's Supper taught by Cornelis Hoen (Honius in Latin) of the Netherlands. Calvin in turn tried to bridge at least in part the gulf between Luther's Real Presence and Zwingli's memorial view.

When Luther was replying to Rome he sounded almost like an Anabaptist. "No faith, no blessing!" he declared. But when he was in controversy with the Anabaptists they feared that he was all too close to Rome in his view of the sacraments. No one gets into the kingdom without the new birth, therefore baptism is also for infants! Luther also used the rather ingenious argument that just as a sleeping man can be a Christian, and therefore have faith, so infants may be said to have "hidden faith" — an argument which the Free Churchmen considered ridiculous. For sleeping people do not hear the gospel, nor do they get converted in their sleep, nor do they make the commitments of baptism in their sleep.

As to the Lord's Supper the error which loomed sky-high for the Anabaptists was the indiscriminate serving of the Lord's Supper to the rank and file of the citizens in a given "parish," whether or not they were living as Christians.

In the course of time the Dutch Anabaptists, led initially by two brothers, Obbe Philips and Dirck Philips, began to observe the ceremony of the basin and the towel (John 13:1-17), and in a generation or so one small Dutch Anabaptist community began to observe foot washing as a church ceremony. Today some Mennonites so observe the teaching of the Lord, while others feel that it was essentially an object lesson on the spirit of love and brotherhood which should characterize the life and attitudes of those in the church of Christ. Those who are convinced of the value of the symbol being literally observed point out how definitely Christ commanded its observance: "If I then your Lord and Master have washed your feet, you also ought to wash one another's feet." He also indicated that not only do believers stand in need of the bath [of regeneration]; they also need daily cleansing as they walk through life in human weakness. Evangelist John S. Coffman therefore suggested in 1891 that the Mennonite Church observes *three principal ordinances:*

baptism, communion, and foot washing. Mennonites also ordain ministers and, of course, they celebrate marriage ceremonies, solemnly bury the dead, anoint the sick with oil, observe the holy kiss of the life of the church, and worship in conformity with the teaching of the New Testament: the men with bared heads, and the women veiled.

Actually John S. Coffman was not closely following Conrad Grebel and Menno Simons in teaching three ordinances — but if he was aware of that fact, it would not have bothered him. For the essence of the Free Church tradition is *to ignore traditional human theology and practice* and in each generation to seek afresh to be wholly faithful to Christ and His Word. And who is to say that today there is no need of a symbol of equality, love, and lowly service in the Christian brotherhood?

If there was anything about which Menno Simons could become almost ecstatic it was the holy joy of the *Eucharist* (the Thanksgiving Meal known as the Lord's Supper). "Oh, delightful assembly and Christian marriage feast," he four times exclaimed in his *Foundation of Christian Doctrine (Writings, p. 148)*. He glories in "the holy mysteries, by means of the visible signs of bread and wine"; he rejoices that "the joyous word of divine grace . . . His glorious benefits, favor, love, service, tears, prayers, His cross and death, are set forth and urged with delightful thanksgiving and devout joy." Further, at the Lord's table, "hungry consciences are fed with the heavenly bread of the divine Word, with the wine of the Holy Ghost," and — to use Menno's vigorous figure — "where the peaceful, joyous souls sing and play before the Lord."

And who shall partake of this joyous celebration? Menno replies: "They are invited who crucify the flesh and are driven by the Holy Spirit; who sincerely believe in God, seek, fear, and love Him, and in their weakness willingly serve and obey Him. For they are members of His body, flesh of His flesh, bone of His bone." Menno held that the Lord's Supper assures us of the remission of our sins; it admonishes us to unity, love, and peace in the church; and it . . . [underscores] that we must be regenerated "to all righteousness, thanksgiving, peace, and joy in the Holy Ghost — to a blameless life" (*Writings*, 150).

3

Christ's Lordship

As we have seen, the Anabaptists regarded Jesus Christ as the center of the Bible, as *the very Word of God* in His person. It was of Him that the prophets wrote. It is to His life, teachings, death, and resurrection that the four *Gospel* writers give their full attention. He is the One who baptized with the Holy Spirit His waiting disciples on the day of Pentecost about AD 30, and who continues to baptize every convert to the Christian faith (Matthew 3:11; Mark 1:8; Luke 3:16; John 1:26, 33; Acts 1:5; 1 Corinthians 12:13). He is the One who led His apostles to write the *Epistles* of the New Testament — those letters of faith and sound instruction which the Christian church has found so helpful in its life and witness. And He is the One who gave to the church that great drama known as the *Revelation* or *Apocalypse*. The earliest Christian confession of faith was undoubtedly the two words JESUS [IS] LORD! (1 Corinthians 12:3, Romans 10:9). It is therefore no wonder when Menno Simons put on the title page of every one of his twenty-five books: "For other foundation can no man lay than that is laid, which is Jesus Christ." Menno declared that those who are regenerated have a spiritual king over them who rules them with "the sceptre of His mouth," that is, with His Spirit and Word (*Writings*, 94).

The Lord's Grace

The Anabaptists were bitterly critical of the low level of Christian life which they observed in sixteenth-century society. All too often the fact that these people had been "christened" seemed to make no difference at all in their way of life. So many people simply gave no evidence of the new birth and the new life which is in Christ Jesus. Too many seemed to feel that they had done their duty if they observed the ceremonies of the church. Such people, cried the Free Churchmen, still stand in need of Christ and His salvation! The state churchmen replied that the Anabaptists were works-saints, self-righteous Pharisees, legalists, and fanatics. (See Leonard Verduin. *The Reformers and their Stepchildren*, Eerdmans, 1964.) The actual truth was that the theologians among the Anabaptists taught salvation by grace just as emphatically as Luther. Over forty times Menno acknowledged his great weakness, and that he could but plead the grace of God. Salvation is wholly of grace. " . . . It is grace, and will be grace to all eternity," Menno insisted. "For Christ's sake we are in grace, for His sake we are heard, and for His sake our faults and failings which are committed against our will are remitted. For it is He who stands between His Father and His imperfect children, with His perfect righteousness. . ." (*Writings*, 506). The Free Churchmen had no quarrel with the Reformers over divine grace.

The Lord's Transformation

The real point of tension between the Anabaptists and the leading Reformers had to do with inner transformation and with a life of holy discipleship. The Anabaptists were aware of the depravity of the flesh; they did not deny their Adamic inheritance. But they had a remarkable optimism — not about human nature, but — about what Christ could do through the Spirit in the lives of His sons and daughters. They will, to be sure, always be aware of their inner need; they will always as true children of God, have a certain "brokenness" of spirit as they realize how far short they fall from full conformity to their Lord's character and will. They therefore rejoiced that Christ Jesus was their adequate and sufficient "mercy seat," as the Luther Bible rendered the Greek in Romans 3:25. Menno's vivid description of his pre-Christian way of life (although an ordained Roman priest, 1524-36) is set forth frankly in his little book, *Meditation on the Twenty-fifth Psalm*. After speaking of his distress of soul

50

brought about by Holy Spirit conviction, he wrote these wholesome words: "And yet the deeper I am grieved, the more I am consoled by Thy Word, for it teaches me Thy mercy, grace, and favor, and the remission of my sins through Christ, Thy beloved Son, our Lord. . . . This promise quiets me. This promise gladdens me" *(Writings,* 77, 78). The doctrine of forgiveness, and of righteousness by faith ("justification") is as much needed by those in the Anabaptist-Mennonite tradition as by any other Christians.

The real difference of opinion centered in the doctrine of sanctification. The Anabaptists, although recognizing that they always stood only by grace, nevertheless believed that Spirit-filled Christians could live a significantly higher level of Christian life than was found in so many members of the state churches. Perhaps Luther, by his correct and powerful attack on works of merit in Romanism, failed to make equally clear that as regenerated and "Spirit-baptized" sons and daughters of God we are *not* always simultaneously justified and sinners *(simul justus et peccator* in Latin). It is a matter of historical record that Luther was grieved in heart in his latter years at the low level of Christian living on the part of so many Evangelicals (Protestants) in Germany. Yet the fact remains that when the Anabaptists, reading passages like Romans 6 and Colossians 3 exulted in their glorious opportunity to be "walking in the resurrection," the leading Reformers accused them of fanaticism pure and simple. Was there on the part of the Anabaptists perhaps also a rather extreme emphasis on their victory in Christ?

Menno could exult: " . . . They are renewed in Christ, and have received a new heart and spirit. Once they were earthly-minded, now heavenly; once they were carnal, now spiritual; once they were unrighteous, now righteous; once they were evil, now good; and they live no longer after the old corrupted nature of the first earthly Adam, but after the new upright nature of the new and heavenly 'Adam,' Christ Jesus. . . . Their poor weak life they daily renew more and more. . . . Their minds are like the mind of Christ, they gladly walk as He walked; they crucify and tame their flesh with all its evil lusts" *(Writings,* 93).

Similarly, Martin Weninger of Schaffhausen, lamented the moral defeatism which he regarded the leading Reformers as teaching: "They teach contrary to Paul (Romans 6) that one cannot be free of sin and live in righteousness: 'One must sin to the grave; no one can keep the commandments of God' (1 John 3, 5) — which is not true!" He went on to quote many passages which stated emphatically that Christians are able in Christ to live holy lives. Christ's redemption is actually effective. Weninger closed his essay by declaring: "The right done from the fear of God is acceptable to God."

Resisting the World's Mold

This doctrine of "walking in the resurrection" meant negatively — to borrow the Phillips paraphrase of Romans 12:2 — that the Anabaptists were firmly minded not to allow the world *to squeeze them into its mold.* They therefore protested not only against such flagrant violations of the moral law of God as fornication, adultery, robbery, and murder; they were also opposed to frequenting drinking establishments, to living in affluence, to following that which they felt was unbecoming in the style of life of those not born again. Observers as early as the first decade of the Anabaptist movement commented, for example, on their plain and simple attire. This protest against wealth and display in one's style of life ultimately came to be called "separation" from or "nonconformity" to the world. Unfortunately, after some centuries, the formalized aspects of nonconformity sometimes tended to be more faithfully maintained than the inner realities which the forms were intended to symbolize and safeguard. (For example, a Mennonite might feel free to purchase the most expensive car available, provided it was black.)

Many youth are now seeking to recapture the very essence of the original protest against living in wealth, affluence, and self-indulgence. Living by the royal law of love dare no longer mean only refusing to take up arms in times of war; it must also mean achieving openness and sincerity and real love in the home and in the church and community. All of life, as the Anabaptists insisted, must be lived under the lordship of Christ. It must all be "sanctified," that is, made Christlike in character.

It should also be emphasized that although symbols of nonconformity can outlive their usefulness, and although if true spirituality is lost such symbols will become substitutes for the reality they are intended to symbolize, yet we dare not despise symbols. The sociologists probably realize this better than the theologians! *Suitable symbols are genuinely helpful in maintaining values and attitudes not shared by the larger society.*

Loving and Suffering Disciples

The Free Churchmen regarded government as one of God's good gifts to society. Following the teaching of the New Testament, they emphasized submission to the government — refusing only to obey when commanded to violate the revealed will of God (Acts 4:19, 20; 5:28, 29). It is the duty of God's children to pay their taxes, and to show respect and honor to governmental authorities (Romans 13:1-7), and also to uphold in prayer those bearing the fearsome

responsibilities and burdens of public office —
with especial concern for liberty of conscience
(1 Timothy 2:1-4). In the event of official governmental efforts to suppress the faith, the children of God can but quietly endure (Revelation
13:10). The pattern of this quiet endurance and
meek acceptance of unjust suffering is the Lord
Jesus Himself, for He quietly lay on the cross
as the Roman soldiers spiked Him down, only
praying for God's forgiveness for the soldiers.
Christ is the example which Christians are to
follow; they are to walk in His footsteps. When
He was reviled and made to suffer, His only
response was to commit Himself to the care of
God, regardless of what it might cost (1 Peter
2:21-23). (It cost Him His life.) And if anyone
wishes to be His disciple, he must take up his
individual cross of unjust suffering — that which
comes to him because He is following Christ
(Luke 9:23-26).

But we are not confined to generalities.
Christ plainly taught that one shall not fight
back when an evil man abuses us. The Old
Testament did allow legal retaliation — and the
code for the judge to impose was "eye for eye"
(Exodus 21:24). But Jesus forbade His followers
any and every sort of retaliation (Matthew 5:
38-42). Yet the Lord also revealed a way to
"overcome" evil men: We shall love them with
the same kind of forgiving love as God mani-
fests to those men and women who reject Him

(Matthew 5:43-48). This means overcoming evil with good (Romans 12:18-21). Although Christians "walk in the flesh" like other people, they do not "war according to the flesh" (2 Corinthians 10:3). It is rather their assignment to render a ministry of reconciliation. They are to speak for God in thus urging men: "We beseech you on behalf of Christ, be reconciled to God" (2 Corinthians 5:20).

Scholars such as C. J. Cadoux have reminded modern Christendom that the church in the early centuries was a nonresistant body. They refused all military service. One of the charges of the pagan Celsus against the Christians in the 170s was that they refused military service. Two generations later the church father Origen (martyred about 254) replied eloquently to Celsus. He admitted that Christians do not indeed take up worldly weapons to fight for the emperor. But Origen insisted that they really did "fight" for the emperor and the welfare of the empire — by forming an "army" of prayer. In AD 295 a North African named Maximilian was executed because he firmly declined as a Christian to serve as a soldier. It was the post-Nicene church which worked out a rationalization which made many Christians comfortable in the Roman legions. The most effective rationale was that of Augustine who in the early 400s stoutly defended participation in a "just war." Since that time most Christians have taken refuge in this position that the war being fought is just — and on *both sides* of the conflict! But the Anabaptists insisted on the basis of what they felt was the plain and clear teaching of Christ and His apostles that they simply could not take up arms against their fellowmen.

Conrad Grebel, the founder of the Free Church, wrote in 1524: "One should also not protect the gospel and its adherents with the sword, nor themselves. . . . True believing Christians are sheep among wolves, sheep for the slaughter. They must be baptized in anxiety, distress, affliction, persecution, suffering, and death. They must pass through the probation of fire, and reach the fatherland of eternal rest, not by slaying their bodily [enemies] but by mortifying their spiritual enemies. They employ neither worldly sword nor war, since with them killing is absolutely renounced" (*wann by inen ist dass toetten gar abgetan,* to cite Grebel's Swiss German). Many dozen similar statements could be quoted from Swiss, German, Dutch, and Austrian Anabaptists. The Historic Peace Churches — Brethren, Friends, Mennonites, and Brethren in Christ — long for the day when Christendom will take a fresh look at the ancient church and discern that it was more faithful than the church of the Middle Ages which, with some notable exceptions, did not hestitate to wage war, and even to utilize force in the "conversion" and baptism of some peoples — Charlemagne and the Saxons, for example.

Christ and the Oath

As we have observed throughout these essays, the Old Testament filled for the Anabaptists a preparatory role. They did not deny that in its basic theology and ethics there are without doubt strong bonds of continuity between the Old and New Testaments — the same human sin and need, the same loving and seeking God, the same need of mediated access to the Father, the same command to live in holiness and love, the same efficacy of prayer, to name some sample areas of truth. And yet the Anabaptists also saw progression and development. What was present in the Old Testament in bud form opens up to full flower in the New. The doctrine of the hereafter is much clearer in the New Covenant, for example. The Free Churchmen therefore rejected what might be called a "Flat Bible" — as if one could set up verses out of the Old Testament with the same finality as one can from Christ and the apostles! We have already noted that this applied to such items as the status of women, divorce, remarriage (see Matthew 19:3-9), polygamy, warfare, and so on.

One of the areas which Christ brought to a full expression of the will of God was the civil oath. The Old Testament allowed the swearing of true oaths in the name of Yahweh, but our Lord said that such swearing is not appropriate for finite creatures — unable as they are even to make one hair grow white or black. God, to be sure, is able to swear to His promises, for He is without reservation able to carry out what He promises to do. But in our limitations of knowledge and strength, we human beings are not like Him. Furthermore, an oath is really an appeal to God to bring His curse upon us if we do not "tell the truth, all the truth, and nothing but the truth." But this is precisely what finite human beings find incompatible with being a creature, says Jesus. See Matthew 5:33-37, and His elaboration on the grounds of His prohibition in Matthew 23:16-22: all oaths, even so-called lesser oaths, ultimately involve God Himself. Such swearing is precisely what Jesus is warning against when He said emphatically: "But I [emphatic ego] say unto you, Swear not at all." We might well ask, If anyone insists that Jesus did not mean what He said, *how could He have said it more clearly?* Compare also James 5:12.

Menno discusses the matter at length on pages 517-521 of his *Complete Writings*. Note also the succinct treatment of oaths in the 1527 Schleitheim *Agreement*.

The Lord of the Conscience

In the judgment of the Free Churchmen, one

of the saddest developments in Germany in the sixteenth century was the setting up (1526 —) of territorial churches — a system in which the ruler of each area determined the official religion of his area. Luther regretfully allowed the princes which became Evangelical to serve as "Emergency Bishops" *(Notbischoefe)* in the territorial Lutheran churches. But how, asked the Free Churchmen, can anyone determine the faith of others? Are we not individually responsible to God? And did not Luther himself stand up against both the pope and the Holy Roman Emperor *on the ground that his conscience was captive to the Word of God?* Regardless of the lamentation of the Anabaptists, the territorial church system was, however, set up. Catholics then persecuted Lutherans; Lutherans persecuted Catholics; and Anglicans, Catholics, Lutherans, and Reformed joined in condemning the Anabaptists as being worthy of death, and handing them over to the "secular," that is, to the governing authorities for execution.

In vain did Menno lament that civil rulers were so willing to obey the imperial mandates against the Anabaptists. In vain did he protest against such sinful shedding of blood. In vain did he protest that it was not right for those who claimed to be spiritual pastors to call upon the secular government to destroy the Free Churchmen by water, fire, and sword. (Menno called such Reformers "men of blood.) All the

Anabaptists could do was to go on quietly insisting that they had "but one Lord and Master of our conscience, Jesus Christ, whose Word, will, commandment, and ordinance, it becomes us as His willing disciples to follow, even as the bride is ready to obey the bridegroom's voice" (*Writings*, 126).

In a solemn protest against the persecuting rulers Menno wrote: "But the reviling, betraying, and agitation of your priests, and your unmerciful mandates and edicts must be our 'scriptures,' and your rackers, hangmen, wrath, torture chambers, water and stake, fire and sword (*O God*), must be our instructors and teachers. . . . How this is to be harmonized with the Spirit, doctrine, and conduct of Christ, and with Christian kindness, love, and friendly spirit, you, my dear sirs, may ponder at some length. This I know for certain, that all bloodthirsty preachers and all rulers who propose and practice these things are not Christ's disciples. . . . It is verily wholly improper, says Cyprian, that such lionlike raving and wolflike fury should dwell in a Christian heart. . . .

"Do not excuse yourselves, dear sirs, and judges, because you are the servants of the emperor. This will not clear you in the day of vengeance. . . .

"Do not usurp the judgment and kingdom of Christ, for He alone is the ruler of the conscience. . . " (*Writings*, 202, 204).

In another context Menno insisted that "we must be governed by the plainly expressed commands of Christ and the pure doctrines and practices of His holy apostles. . ." (*Writings*, 129).

And who is this person who alone is Lord of the conscience? Menno attempts to put into the mouth of his Lord His self-denying love: "I left the glory of my Father, and came into this sad world as a poor slave to save you. For I saw that you all belonged to the devil, and that there was none to redeem you; that you had all gone astray like erring sheep, and there was none who cared for you . . . and there was none that could heal you. Therefore did I come from heaven, and became a poor, weak, and dying man, in all things like unto you, sin excepted. In my great love I sought you out with zeal, found you miserable, sorrowful, yes, half-dead. The services of my love I have demonstrated heartily toward you; your sores I bandaged; your blood I wiped away; wine and oil I have poured into your putrid wounds; set you free from the jaws of the hellish beasts; I took you upon my shoulders and led you into the tabernacles of peace. Your nakedness I covered; I had compassion on your misery; the law I have fulfilled for you; your sins I took away. The peace, grace, and favor of my Father I proclaimed to you; His good will I revealed; the way of truth I pointed out; and I have powerfully testified to you by my marvelous signs and great miracles that I am the true Messiah, the promised Prince and Saviour" *(Writings,* 147).

Still a Live Issue

The struggles of conscience with the several governments of the world are not yet fully resolved. Various nations — United States, Canada, Mexico, Paraguay, Great Britain, West Germany, France, the Netherlands, to name a few — have now made legal provision for conscientious objectors to military service. For this the Historic Peace Churches, and many humanitarian and civil liberties groups, are deeply grateful. International Law also seems to be making slow strides toward a deeper recognition of man's obligation to follow what might be called the light of conscience. Article 8 of the Charter of the International Military Tribunal which conducted the Nuremberg trials of those Germans accused of war crimes during World War II specifically declared that a defendant was not exempt from prosecution on the ground that he had acted upon order of his government or of a superior. On the contrary, he was to be held responsible for his "crimes," even though they were "legal" in his land. In other words, *Befehl ist Befehl* (which might be paraphrased, "A command must be obeyed") will not grant a man immunity to do that which is intrinsically wrong — that is, that which the international community regards as a crime.

Would it not be a major step forward to recognize a man's God-given obligation to live up to the light of his conscience whether or not either national or an international legal consensus happens to be in agreement with him? Is there not something both sacred and sovereign about one's obligation to follow his conscience? May not the Anabaptists have been right when they insisted that they could not allow the emperor or the imperial mandates to guide them, and not even the learned theologians of the territorial churches? Were they not perhaps right in the conviction for which they were willing to die: Christ and He alone is Lord of the conscience?

This principle still has its suffering adherents. There are men in prison today who are there because they felt impelled by conscience to refuse any and all cooperation with the giant military machine which their land is operating. Some of these men have been granted judicial leniency and have been assigned to humanitarian service along the lines upon which the Mennonite Central Committee and similar organizations operate. But others have been imprisoned because they dared to follow conscience in absolute obedience.

O Christ, be near to those
who suffer because they seek to
follow Thee!